DEVOTIONS FROM A
Shattered Heart

Kimber Lyn

ISBN 979-8-89130-038-5 (paperback)
ISBN 979-8-89130-039-2 (digital)

Christian Faith Publishing
832 Park Avenue
Meadville, PA 16335
www.christianfaithpublishing.com

Printed in the United States of America

My name is Kimber Lyn.

This is my journey—a journey that comes from a shattered heart many times over, from my personal choices, from others' choices, and, of course, from life itself and the result of living in a fallen world. There is no perfection on this side of eternity. I, like you, am just a woman seeking God with her whole heart, shattered pieces and all. May the lessons learned from my own shattered heart bring you comfort and direct you to the Lord God of all creation, who is the only one who can truly heal our shattered hearts. He is the only one who can truly free us from the chains that we are bound with of our own choosing when we choose our will over God's. May God' blessings be upon you as you read my journey, and may God free you from your own chains and heal your own shattered heart as you turn to Him and choose daily to follow God's will for your life and not your own. I guarantee this decision will change your life as it did mine.

Lessons Learned

Through rejection, I have learned acceptance.
Through poor choices, I have learned redemption.
Through trials, I have learned joy.
Through times of need, I have learned contentment.
Through fear, I have learned peace.
Through motherhood, I have learned love.
Through betrayal, I have learned forgiveness.
Through pain, I have learned compassion.
My heavenly necklace—inspired by Karen Marjoris-Garrison's story of the pearls of time necklace told by her friend and mentor Sarah—from *Women Living with Purpose…God's Way.*

Rejection and Acceptance

As I look back through experiences that have shattered my heart, I find myself looking back toward my childhood. It was in childhood that my heart started to break although I was not aware of it at the time. I come from a blended family, and although I knew my parents loved me, there were experiences during that season that caused me to feel rejected. It was through my father's sister in that beautiful, messed up, and very real family that I grew up in that I discovered acceptance—through the love of Jesus Christ underneath a tree—as she taught me about God and His Son and the sacrifice that was made for me. And yet, even with that decision to accept Christ into my life, I still continued to live a life of rejection instead of acceptance well into my adult years.

Looking back, I believe I am just now learning what God's acceptance truly is and to understand that I was created with a purpose. I have begun to allow the fact to believe that God knew all of my days, all of my experiences and choices before I was even born yet He accepted me and died for me anyway. Because that is who God is. It is through the Lord alone that we have our true identity and are accepted and loved unconditionally for who we truly are, warts and all. Psalm 139:1–23 AMP says it best and is a psalm I turn to often when I am feeling most rejected and unacceptable in mine, others, and even God's eyes:

> O Lord, you have searched
> me [thoroughly] and have known
> me.

God's love has searched my heart and soul and knows it all.

> You know when I sit down
> and when I rise up [my entire
> life, everything I do];
> You understand my thought
> from afar.

God's love watches my every move and gives me protection when I rise and when I sleep. He knows every thought, even those in the deep and dark recesses of my mind. He loves me enough to seek me out and hold me accountable and to love me through my choices, good and bad.

> You scrutinize my path and
> my lying down,
>> And You are intimately
> acquainted with all my ways.

God's love seeks me out and chooses to be intimately involved in every aspect of my life.

> Even before there is a word
> on my tongue [still unspoken],
>> Behold, O LORD, You know
> it all.

God's love is acutely aware of my challenges in speaking first and dealing with consequences later, teaching me to slow down and think before I speak.

> You have enclosed me
> behind and before,
>> And [You have] placed Your
> hand upon me.

God's protection is all around me, even when I am feeling alone. He never leaves me.

Such [infinite] knowledge is
too wonderful for me;
It is too high [above me], I
cannot reach it.

There are many times that my mind cannot grasp the enormity of His love for me, the strength of His protection, and the bounty of His provision.

Where can I go from Your
Spirit?
Or where can I flee from
Your presence?

There is nowhere that God's love, protection, and provision cannot find me.

If I ascend to heaven, You
are there;
If I make my bed in Sheol
(the nether world, the place of
the dead), behold, You are there.

I can be on the highest mountain filled with joy or the deepest valley filled with despair, and my God will always find me.

> If I take the wings of the
> dawn,
> If I dwell in the remotest
> part of the sea,

If I am flying free with my Lord or in the deepness of my sin...

> Even there Your hand will
> lead me,
> And Your right hand will
> take hold of me.

Like a shepherd with his sheep that has gone astray, my God is always there to lead me back to where I belong.

> If I say, "Surely the darkness
> will cover me,
> And the night will be the
> only light around me,"

With love and mercy, God is there in my darkest hour.

> Even the darkness is not dark to You *and* conceals nothing from You,
> But the night shines as bright as the day;
> Darkness and light are alike *to You.*

God's light shines through my darkness and lights the path I am to take. It surrounds me and fills me.

> For You formed my innermost parts;
> You knit me [together] in my mother's womb.

God has created me for a purpose and knows who I am and who I am to be before I was even born.

> I will give thanks *and* praise to You, for I am fearfully and wonderfully made;
> Wonderful are Your works,

And my soul knows it very
well.

*Thank you, God of heaven and earth, Lord of
my life, for creating me as a unique individual with a
specific purpose.*

My frame was not hidden
from You,
When I was being formed
in secret,
And intricately *and* skill-
fully formed [as if embroidered
with many colors] in the depths
of the earth.

*Thank you, Lord, for creating me as a beautiful
and useful creature in and for your kingdom.*

Your eyes have seen my
unformed substance;
And in Your book were all
written
The days that were
appointed *for me,*

When as yet there was not
one of them [even taking shape].

*Thank You, Father God, for Your plan for my life
and Your care for every detail, from my birth to my death*

How precious also are Your
thoughts to me, O God!
How vast is the sum of
them!

*How I long to know your thoughts and make them
mine, to have more of you and less of me.*

If I could count them, they
would outnumber the sand.
When I awake, I am still
with You.

*When I am overwhelmed with the enormity of
who You are, You are there.*

O that You would kill the
wicked, O God;
Go away from me, there-
fore, men of bloodshed.

*In my hour of need, You protect me from those who
wish to cause me harm.*

> For they speak against You
wickedly,
> Your enemies take *Your
name* in vain.
> Do I not hate those who
hate You, O LORD?
> And do I not loathe those
who rise up against You?
> I hate them with per-
fect *and* utmost hatred;
> They have become my
enemies.

My enemies have become your enemies.

> Search me [thoroughly], O
God, and know my heart;
> Test me and know my anx-
ious thoughts;

*Lord, You know me and my every thought. You test
me for Your good purpose.*

> And   see   if   there   is   any
> wicked *or* hurtful way in me,
>> And lead me in the everlast-
> ing way.

You lead me away from anything that can hurt me or cause me to stray.

Such a comfort this psalm is to me, and yet, even with a life that has been filled with God's provision and protection, there are days when I still feel rejected and alone. I think that is part of my journey—to lean into the Lord for acceptance, unconditional love, and freedom from rejection daily. For He and He alone accepts me for who I am and who I am yet to be. For He created me, and He created you. Today, join me in leaning into the God of love, who accepts you for all the beauty you are now and you are yet to be.

Questions to Ponder

1. When have you felt rejected and alone?
2. What did you do to process those feelings?
3. Did it help or make things worse?
4. How and why?
5. Did you include God in the process?
6. Why or why not?
7. Looking back, what would you do differently?

Poor Choices and Redemption

As I continue to reflect on my life and how far God has brought me, I discover a recurring theme. A theme of poor choices made from my human need to be in control and to do things my way instead of God's. I see a woman who, despite knowing Christ, has continually made the same or similar choices along her life's path. Yes, there have been seasons of growth but oh, so many seasons of failure. In my need for control, I have made poor choices in relationships that have not only hurt me but hurt my children. In my need to do things my way, I have made poor choices in finances that have taken me into debt. In my need for comfort, I have made poor choices in the care of my body, heart, and soul. All these choices have consequences, and all of them have brought me to my knees. But most of all, these choices have brought me to a place where God can redeem me, time and time again. I think I am just now beginning to grasp a little bit of what that redemption looks like yet know it will most likely take a lifetime to really get what God's redemption is and what it cost Him to redeem me and all of humanity from our sinful lives. One of my favorite psalms speaks to this:

> *I waited patiently and* **expectantly for the** LORD; *And He inclined to me and heard my cry. He brought me up out of a horrible pit [of tumult and of destruction], out of the miry clay, And He set my feet upon a rock, steadying my footsteps and establishing my path. He put a new song in my mouth, a song of praise to our God; Many will see and fear [with great reverence] And will trust confidently in the* LORD. Psalm 40:1–3 (AMP)

There are three things I take away from these verses. The first is that when I call out and wait upon the Lord, He hears me and answers my cry, but when I get impatient and do things my way and in my time, He lets me stumble and fall until I am ready to listen and learn at His feet. You would think that after years of making the same choices and having the same or similar consequences, I would have learned this lesson, yet I continue to fall and I continue to fail. I continue to need God's reminders that He is in control, not I.

The second takeaway for me is that even when I fall into the pit of my own making, when I get bogged down in the miry clay of my sin, He always lifts me up, sets my feet upon the rock of His foundation, and, once again, sets me on His path for my life. It doesn't matter how often or how deep or how thick that mud is; God always pulls me up and gets me out. No matter how shaky the ground is beneath my feet, He always sets me on His firm rock of redemption and salvation. He always sets me back on the right path and takes my hand or even carries me when necessary to accomplish His will in my life.

My third take away is that He always gives me a new song of salvation to sing and to share with others what He has done in my life. For it is through my failures and my trials and my weaknesses that God shows Himself to others and leads them to Himself. Because of this, I can confidently trust that nothing is wasted, not a single tear is ignored, and not a single step is missed when I wait expectantly on the Lord, my God.

I am so thankful that my God is a God of redemption. Through redemption by the death of His beloved Son on the cross, He shows just how much He loves and wants the best for us. It is up to us to make the choice to allow Him to give us His best and not to be content with our best, which cannot even begin to match what God has planned for us. To help me remember this lesson, I have written a redemption prayer at different times in my life. Here is my current one. May it bless you and help you to allow God's redemptive love to fill your heart and keep you on God's path and not your own.

Release—my sin, guilt and shame over poor choices and
 accept your gift of forgiveness that I may
Encourage—others to do the same, that we may
 experience the removal of our
Debt—of sin that was washed away by the blood of the
 cross. May I
Envision—Your heart in all things that I may
Merge—my thoughts and feelings into Your
Plan—and not my own; in Your
Time—and not mine. May my life
Inspire—others to follow
Only—You and no one or anything else that may tempt
 us in the here and
Now—that we may always live in the present moment
 and release our past and trust our future to You.
Amen

Questions to Ponder:

1. When have you made poor choices?
2. What did you do to resolve or correct those choices?
3. Did it help or make things worse?
4. How and why?
5. Did you go to the Lord for forgiveness and redemption?
6. Why or why not?
7. Did you ask forgiveness from anyone you may have harmed because of those choices?
8. Why or why not?
9. Looking back, what would you do differently?

Trials and Joy

Whom have I in heaven but you? And there is nothing on earth that I desire besides you. My flesh and my heart may fail, but God is the strength of my heart and my portion forever.
                            —Psalm 73:25–26

My life, like most others, has been filled with trials. These trials have come in many shapes and sizes and have lasted for various lengths of time. When I reflect on them, I find a recurring theme. In all of them, without exception, I felt the presence of God. Not one single time did I feel alone. God was always right there beside me. This does not mean that I was always in a good place in these trials. I remember one time when we thought we were going to lose my precious youngest son to complications of Crohn's disease. I fought with God over my child, questioning why this had to happen. Yet in the end, through many tears and, ultimately, exhaustion I was able to release him to the Lord and trust Him for the outcome, even if it meant God taking him home sooner than I would have liked. I cannot say that at that moment I felt joy, but I can say I felt tremendous peace, which ultimately turned to joy when my son turned the corner the following day and began to improve.

I have found that joy is not being externally happy but feeling internally content and at peace with our circumstances. The peace I felt after the battle with God over my son was also a feeling of contentment of knowing that no matter the outcome, my son was safe in the arms of the Lord. Isn't that what life is about? We will have trials and many storms, but if we lean into the Lord and learn to trust Him for the outcome—whatever that may be—we can be truly content and at peace with the outcome. Not because circumstances change as they do not always do so, such as now, when I am facing a whole other trial with my son regarding his mental health instead of his physical health. There is no change in these present circumstances; my son is still struggling, still making poor choices, and is still living away from me. My circumstances have not changed, but my outlook has. I am learning to be content, to have a sense of joy in knowing that God's got this. He already knows the outcome, and He will not let my son fall any further than he needs to fall to be able to look up and reach for the only one who can save him—our Lord and Savior, Jesus Christ. For the Bible tells us that all have sinned and fallen short of the glory of God and that the only way to true fulfillment and life eternal is through His Son, Jesus Christ.

God is there for me; God is there for my son, and He is there for you. The choice is ours. Do we want to live our lives troubled and weighed down by our sin and choices, or do we want the freedom of life in Christ that He offers? Do we want to let the trials get to us, or let God get to the trial? As for me, I choose joy, no matter the circumstances; I choose faith despite the difficulties; I choose to let God fight my battles and trust Him for the outcome, no matter what that may be.

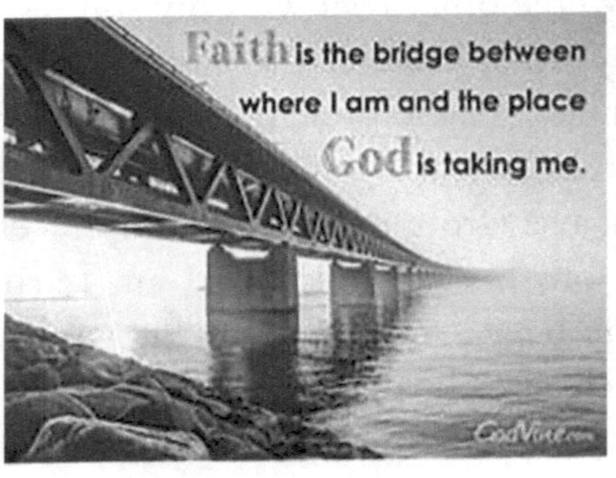

Questions to Ponder

1. What trials have you faced that have caused you to falter or question your faith?
2. How did you respond to the trial?
3. Did it help or make things worse?
4. How and why?
5. Did you go to the Lord with your questions and your tears?
6. Why or why not?
7. Ultimately, did you choose joy over the pain?
8. Why or why not?
9. Looking back, what would you do differently?

Needs and Contentment

I know how to get along and live humbly [in difficult times], and I also know how to enjoy abundance and live in prosperity. In any and every circumstance I have learned the secret [of facing life], whether well-fed or going hungry, whether having an abundance *or being in need. I can do all things [which He has called me to do] through Him who strengthens and* empowers me [to fulfill His purpose—I am self-sufficient in Christ's sufficiency; I am ready for anything and equal to anything through Him who infuses me with inner strength and confident peace.]

—Philippians 4:12–13 AMP

I have had many seasons of need in my life, mostly as a result of poor choices in one of my biggest growth areas: financial management. To say that I don't have a Midas touch would be an understatement! But through it all, God has taught to me to trust in Him for all my needs, big or small, and not once has He let me down. I have always paid the bills, even though till recently, they were usually late. There has always been a roof over our head and food on the table, even one of my famous $5 meals (the kids' favorite mac 'n' cheese with little smokies); always had clothes on our back, even if mostly were from goodwill or hand-me-downs; and when I planned well, such as back-to-school shopping to Target or Walmart specials.

We always found time to spend as a family with movie and game nights, weekend camping trips, and the occasional camping vacation. Annual passes to the zoo and the occasional Disney day were great gifts. We celebrated birthdays with homemade cakes and 99 cents store gift bags, and we always found a way to squeeze at least one special gift out at Christmas from the kids' Santa list.

We also always found a way to give back, whether it was $20 on Christmas day to our single-mom waitress, anonymous baked treats to neighbors, toys for TOTS birthday parties, or fundraiser's for Crohn's and Colitis foundation triathlons. Yet even with all of that provision, the hardest lesson for me was to learn to be content in all things, especially during the many times I wasn't sure how bills were going to get paid, yet they always were.

I think it really hit home for me when my son was so sick and I could not work as much as I wanted to, and yet help came for us from everywhere—and I mean everywhere. And again, when my second marriage ended and I had no idea where I was going to live or how I was going to be able to afford to support myself and my son and keep adequate health insurance for us both. Both of those times were day by day, moments of trusting the Lord for *everything*! They were both probably the hardest seasons of my life next to being a single mom after my first marriage ended with two girls under the age of five. But unlike that first time when I stressed over everything, this time I had no choice but to trust the Lord, God finally was able to bring me to a place of peace, and I didn't even have a place to live at the time. But I knew God did. I learned a lot of hard lessons during those seasons, but the one I hope to have learned and will hold onto is contentment, no matter what trials I may be facing because God has it and He has me. Nothing else matters.

Questions to Ponder

1. What in your life has caused you to struggle with contentment?
2. How did you respond?
3. Did it help or make things worse?
4. How and why?
5. Did you go to the Lord to ask Him to give you contentment, no matter what the circumstance?
6. Why or why not?
7. Are you able to have true contentment now despite your circumstances?
8. Why or why not?
9. Looking back, what would you do differently?

Fear and Peace

And the peace of God [that peace which reassures the heart, that peace] which transcends all understanding, [that peace which] stands guard over your hearts and your minds in Christ Jesus [is yours].

—Philippians 4:7

I am, by nature, a fearful person. My whole life has been a battle with my fears, most of which usually are irrational. I conquered one of my biggest fears when I learned to swim (not just be "water safe") when I participated in a triathlon for team challenge to raise funds and awareness for Crohn's and Colitis diseases when my son was first diagnosed. (By the way, I was fifty years old, so don't use age as an excuse to move forward in something God is asking you to do.) To say I was petrified of swimming in the ocean was an understatement. Then there is this little thing I have about putting my face under water (still working on that one). Both factors could have kept me from not being successful in this event. Yet every time I chose to act in faith and trust God with my safety for that day's training and ultimately the triathlon itself, I gained more confidence and more peace with each successful swim.

As I look back at that time, I realize that has been the way with all my fears. Once I chose to give them to the Lord and step out in faith as I trusted Him to help me conquer it, I not only succeeded but gained confidence and peace with each success. Now, I will never be a world class swimmer, I swam the side stroke for all five hundred meters due to my continued fear and inability to put my face underwater. But I finished and I did it three years in a row! I did not finish first, I was second to last on my first year and the last on my second year due to a fall on my bike, but I did it. You see, God will give us the tools we need to face our fears, and He won't have us handle them all at once. He helps us through one fear at a time, one step at a time. We learn to trust Him with that fear, then He helps us through the next and the next and the next.

*W*HEN WE PUT OUR PROBLEMS IN GOD'S HANDS, HE PUTS HIS PEACE IN OUR HEARTS.

Questions to Ponder

1. What is your biggest fear?
2. How do you deal with that fear?
3. Does it help or make things worse?
4. How and why?
5. Did you go to the Lord to ask Him to help you overcome that fear?
6. Why or why not?
7. Are you able to begin trusting Him to help you overcome that fear now?
8. Why or why not?
9. If you have conquered a fear with the Lord in the past, what makes that situation different from this one?
10. What can you learn about handling your fears from previous success in trusting the Lord to help you overcome them?

Love and Motherhood

And now there remain: faith [abiding trust in God and His promises], hope [confident expectation of eternal salvation], love [unselfish love for others growing out of God's love for me], these three [the choicest graces]; but the greatest of these is love.

—1 Corinthians 13:13

Motherhood has been one of my greatest challenges and yet one of my greatest rewards. I have learned what it means to truly love unconditionally and only have an inkling of what it must have felt like for Mary to watch her Son die for her and the world—past, present, and future.

One of the biggest lessons I have learned is how differently each of us experience how we give love and how we receive love. By God's unique design in our physical appearance, He also gave us unique personalities and temperaments that cause us to give and receive love in different ways. Finding out how to love each child as an individual and yet equally to their siblings is a lesson all its own. It seemed as soon as I thought I had figured it out, their tastes would change, their interests would change, or they had learned a new set of skills that required me to tweak how I chose to love and discipline them. Because discipline is a part of love.

God disciplines us when we stray, and it is our responsibility as a mother to love our children enough to discipline them as well. If we do not teach our children how to love through respect, tolerance, acceptance, and gratitude for what we have, we will be raising disrespectful, self-entitled, indifferent, and intolerant adults. The best way to teach our children this type of love is by example. I failed miserably in that department more times than I can count. But when we fail, that is when we get to teach grace, forgiveness, and unconditional love. We do this by acknowledging our mistakes and not only asking our children to forgive us, but teaching them to pray for God's forgiveness as well by choosing to pray together when conflict arises.

Our children need to see their parents have conflict and them resolving it in a loving and godly way. If they don't see it, they won't learn it, and if they don't learn it, they won't do it. If we are not modeling this type of love and yet we are preaching it, we are sending our children mixed messages that teach it's okay to expect others to love and treat you in a respectful manner, but you don't have to do so in return. And that, my friends, is a very slippery slope that will come back to haunt you in the adolescent years and beyond.

We must always turn to the perfect parent to teach and guide us on how to love and raise children who love and honor God as well as others and themselves. That perfect parent is God, and no other and our children must understand this as well. They must learn that we, too, are human and make mistakes, but only by modeling love, accountability, and forgiveness will we truly be able to grow ourselves into the godly women and mothers God intends us to be as we teach our children how to grow into happy, healthy, productive, and respectful adults, who love and honor God in all they say and do.

Questions to Ponder

1. What are your memories of childhood and your parents style of parenting?
2. What can you take away from your experiences to be a good parent to your children?
3. As a parent, how do you model unconditional love and forgiveness balanced by discipline and accountability?
4. Where do you go to get advice in a difficult parenting situation?
5. Is God your first choice, or is it someone else?
6. Are you able to be accountable to your children to model a loving relationship with your spouse and one that deals with conflict in a healthy and godly manner?
7. Why or why not?
8. Looking back, at your parenting, whether it be one year or eighteen, what would you do differently?

Through Betrayal, I Have Learned Forgiveness

Then Peter came to Him and asked, "Lord, how many times will my brother sin against me and I forgive him and let it go? Up to seven times?" Jesus answered him, "I say to you, not up to seven times, but seventy times seven."

—Matthew 18:21–22 (AMP)

Forgiveness. I struggle so much with this. Forgiving those who have hurt and betrayed me. I don't know why this is so difficult and why it takes me so long to process the pain and then forgive and let it go. It feels unnatural. It is not comfortable. It doesn't seem right. Yet in God's world, forgiveness is key. He made the greatest sacrifice of all so that He could forgive us our sins, and yet we—or at least I—cannot seem to forgive others as easily as He forgives us. Our pride, our self-righteousness, our own personal agenda—all of it gets in the way of forgiveness, especially when it is a betrayal from someone we love. I know for me, this is the hardest to forgive, and I keep replaying it over and over in my mind. I can't seem to move on. I get stuck in the mud of why, and woe is me to be treated this way.

Funny thing about forgiveness, though, is once I do it, I am free. It doesn't matter if the person asked for it or if I even told them personally. When I pray through forgiveness for someone who has hurt me deeply and has betrayed my trust, there is freedom in the release of all that junk that was holding me back, keeping me stuck in the mud or down on the ground, beaten and whimpering. When I choose to forgive, I choose to let it go. I choose to not let it hold me anymore. I choose to get up to fight another day. I choose to live, and I choose to love.

Forgiveness is freedom. Forgiveness is love. Forgiveness is faith. Forgiveness is peace. Forgiveness is God in action in us, day in and day out, no matter what people say, no matter what people do. We are to forgive as Christ forgave us, and it is through that forgiveness that He sets us free whether it is for our sins or us forgiving someone for their sin against us. Forgiveness is freedom.

Forgiveness is not always easy. At times, it feels more painful than the wound we suffered, to forgive the one that inflicted it. And yet, there is no peace without forgiveness.

Questions to Ponder

1. When have you found it hard to forgive someone?
2. What helped you to be able to finally forgive them?
3. As a believer, why do you think it is so important for us to forgive others?
4. How does the Bible help us learn to forgive?
5. Do you regularly ask God for forgiveness when you have committed a wrong act, said a wrong word, or watched or listened to something you shouldn't have?
6. Why or why not?

7. Who can you turn to help for both asking forgiveness of God and others and giving forgiveness?

8. Is there someone that God is asking you to forgive or someone He is telling you to ask for forgiveness?

9. If so, go now and forgive as Christ forgave you and ask for forgiveness if you are the one who has committed the wrong, both of God and the one you hurt.

Through Pain, I Have Learned Compassion

He heals the brokenhearted.
And binds up their wounds [healing their
pain and comforting their sorrow].

—Psalm 147:3 (AMP)

Pain—we all experience it at some point in our lives, and for many of us, more than once. Pain comes in a variety of forms—some physical, some emotional or mental, some caused by our own choices and other pain caused by choices made by those we love or might not even know. I know one thing that is common in all: pain, no matter where it comes from or what it is, it hurts. Pain is real, it is palpable, and it must be worked through and dealt with because it isn't going anywhere until we do. I have experienced physical pain from medical issues, mental and emotional pain from my choices and the choices of others, but in it all, God has taught me one thing: compassion and empathy for others who are hurting. And He has given me a gift for helping others work through their pain that I would not have had without experiencing my own.

We of this world can be so self-centered and think that everything revolves around us, that no one else has gone through what we are or can understand and relate to our pain, and that is in part true. But pain does have a common denominator—it hurts. And it hurts a lot. I know of one person who has experienced more pain than I ever have or probably ever will, and that is my Lord, Jesus Christ. He suffered tremendous pain and suffering through the beatings, and ultimately, His death on the cross. I know of no other person who gets what I am feeling when I hurt physically or emotionally. It is true that some pain will not end until we reach the other side of eternity, and we must walk in it daily sometimes, but there is another pain that, as we walk through it with our Lord, He has lessons for us to learn that we could learn no other way.

For me, that lesson was compassion and empathy. It is being able to look at someone else's pain and know what to say or what not to say. It is knowing that all I can really do is point them to my Lord and Savior, Jesus Christ, the ultimate healer of all our wounds, great and small. For in this life, we will experience pain, but Christ is there to take it away, here or in eternity. Either way, He is the only one who can heal and mend our broken hearts and bodies. It is to Him I cling, it is to Him I turn, and it is in Him I trust.

Won't you join me in giving all your pain and all your heartache to the ultimate physician of our body and souls, Jesus Christ? And the next time you see someone struggling, remember we all have pain and their pain is as real to them as yours is to you. Won't you stand beside them as so many have stood beside you? Instead of judging their pain against yours, help them to leave their pain at the altar alongside of yours, be a blessing to someone who is hurting today, show them the empathy and compassion of our Lord and Savior, who gave all that we might live.

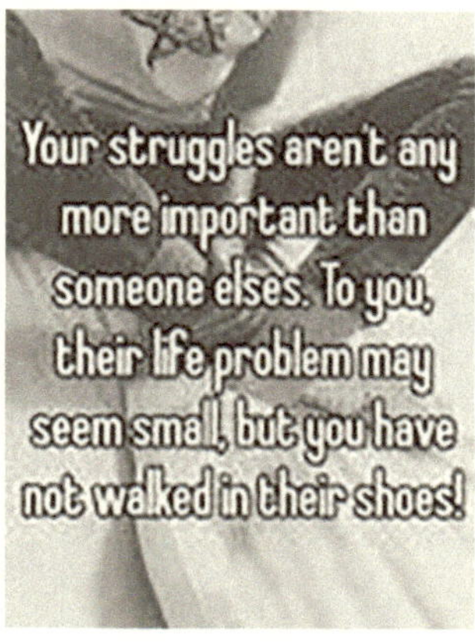

Questions to Ponder

1. When have you experienced compassion?
2. When have you shown compassion to someone?
3. As a believer why do you think it so important for us to show compassion?
4. How does the Bible help us learn how to show compassion?
5. Do you find it hard to show compassion?
6. Why or why not?
7. What are some ways that you can begin to show more compassion to those around you at home, work, church, and community?

About the Author

Kimber Lyn is a woman seeking after God's own heart in her daily life. She lives in Escondido, California, with her sweet cat Cosmo and is a mother of grown children. She enjoys being outside whenever she can, especially at the ocean, and loves to read. Living for the Lord is her passion, and helping others to discover the joy of a living and breathing relationship with the ultimate healer, Our Lord and Savior Jesus Christ, is her life mission.